TIGER FACING THE MIST

Pauline Stainer is a freelance writer and tutor. After many years in rural Essex and then on the Orkney island of Rousay, she now lives at Hadleigh in Suffolk. Her Bloodaxe titles include *The Lady & the Hare: New & Selected Poems* (2003), which draws on five previous books, as well as a new collection, *A Litany of High Waters*, and two later collections, *Crossing the Snowline* (2008) and *Tiger Facing the Mist* (2013). Along with *The Lady & the Hare*, her collections *The Honeycomb*, *Sighting the Slave Ship* and *The Ice-Pilot Speaks* were all Poetry Book Society Recommendations. Her fourth collection *The Wounddresser's Dream* was shortlisted for the Whitbread Poetry Award in 1996. Pauline Stainer received a 2009 Cholmondeley Award for her poetry.

PAULINE STAINER

TIGER FACING THE MIST

BLOODAXE BOOKS

ISBN: 978 1 85224 954 0

First published 2013 by
Bloodaxe Books Ltd,
Highgreen,
Tarset,
Northumberland NE48 1RP.

www.bloodaxebooks.com
For further information about Bloodaxe titles
please visit our website or write to
the above address for a catalogue.

Supported by
**ARTS COUNCIL
ENGLAND**

Cover design: Neil Astley & Pamela Robertson-Pearce.

Printed in Great Britain by
Bell & Bain Limited, Glasgow, Scotland.

For Ruth, Joshua, Danny, Heather, Charlotte, and Harriet

*

'Margins are best'

MARK COCKER

'but her *face* like that of the *Annuntiata* expects
the Pencill of an Angell'

THOMAS VAUGHAN

ACKNOWLEDGEMENTS

Acknowledgements are due to the editors of the following publications in which these poems first appeared: *The Frogmore Papers, London Magazine, Modern Poetry in Translation, Poetry Ireland Review, Resurgence* and *The Warwick Review.*

'The Queen of Sutton Hoo' was published in *The Sutton Hoo Festival Anthology 2009*; 'The Elephants of Atlantis' was published in T*he Review of Contemporary Poetry*; (blue chrome publishing, 2005); 'Momentum' appeared in *The King's Lynn Silver Folio: Poems for Tony Ellis*, a limited edition edited by Michael Hulse (2009).

'Insight' was one of the prize-winning poems at Warwick University's International symposium on Poetry and Medicine 2010. 'A Kind of Quickening' was commissioned by The Poetry Society to celebrate the 40th Anniversary of The Churches Conservation Trust and was read at their service in Westminster Abbey on 16 September 2009.

CONTENTS

9 Tiger facing the mist
10 Reading by snowlight
11 On whiteness
12 The mirror in the orchard
13 Hares at dusk
14 Caliban and the blue moon
15 Against hesitancy
16 Peregrini
17 Qaumaneq
18 Conjuration
19 The nature of the game
20 Momentum
21 The impulse
22 Looking to Borrowdale
23 The blue planet
24 Shibui
25 After long fallow
26 Overspill
27 The owl window
28 On opening the north door
30 The mole-catcher's cottage
31 Orkney Epiphany
32 The sheep-rustling
33 In praise of flying squirrels
34 The elephants of Atlantis
36 How the snow-leopard became
37 Suffolk albatross
38 The Queen of Sutton Hoo
39 The beekeepers
40 The Druids of Primrose Hill
41 Mountain bikers

42   After Ernst

43   The lay clerk's song

44   Sea-otter and child

45   Our Lady of the dry tree

46   Krishna and the milkmaids

47   Outsleeping the monsoon

48   The dislocation

50   Insight

52   George Herbert plays the lute

53   The sounding

54   Overwintering

55   Onsen

56   The wedding at Valletta

58   Rimbaud in Zanzibar

59   Apothecary's song

60   A Kind of Quickening

62   Long Friday

63   The key and the crystal

Tiger facing the mist

Real or imagined –
those grey stripes
moving
through mountain mist
with a sense of music?

This is the art
of passing-through,
to the cry of
a crouching deer
come and gone.

Not how to vanish,
for the tiger's eye
becomes amber
underground,
but the magical threshold

between cargoes of dust –
while far below,
Lady Murasaki's maids
make snowballs
in the moonlit garden.

Reading by snowlight

I want to take the weight
out of language
the way snowfall
on the red planet
vaporises before settling

outside,
everything is moccasined,
the ground suddenly consecrated
as if something else
is being said

the air smokeless
with pure-white candles
from the sperm whale,
even the juniper
wonderfully anonymous

nothing within earshot
except voices
gentling each other
along the page
like silver foxes.

Queer, this effect
of snow on the psyche,
words waiting to happen,
the snowfields beyond
untranslatable.

On whiteness

Birch trees
quilled in the lake,
white-phase gyrfalcons
so pale
they are subliminal.

If white light
says so much,
why do we wait
for the moon
to throw a shadow

like none other?

The mirror in the orchard

It is not quite dark –
there is enough light
to reflect a company of birds
roosting, roosting
in the moonlit mirror.

In the frost after dawn,
when sap runs bright blue
and the sun comes up
as sharpshooter,
you remember

the discovered snow
of their breasts
in the apple tree,
the way they shimmered
like satin, even in shade.

Hares at dusk

They give nothing away
in the lesser dark,
the varying hares

their focus
the shuttered blues
between pasture and late snow.

It is mesmerising
how many things go missing
at the witching hour

only a waterworn moon
and the rippling machinery
of the moment

still holding the light.

Caliban and the blue moon

Perhaps it was the second
full moon in one month
that unsettled me,
for I began to dream
of forsaking the island.

You would think
I had everything –
painted quails,
flying frogs
that change colour at night

but I'd become
a creature of habit,
for when a ship moored
with swallows gathered
on its shrouds

I watched the way
dew lay on their wings
all night,
and felt that grievous
enchantment

the electricity of exile.

Against hesitancy

White on white.
Under the snow
Chinese musicians
still play
to their dancing geese.

Outer and inner
landscapes,
the perilous process
of what you do
with what you see

like that moment
unreadable as dewfall,
when we watched
men from the observatory
release young sea-eagles
into the drizzle.

Peregrini

Solitary, devout,
they settle on remote islands
knowing patience is deeper
over great moss.

Occasionally, between
the lapsed psalms
and floating sweet grass
they hear muffled depth-charges

as if the horizons
they jettisoned
for darkening fugues
of salt and sleet

begin to close
on their snow-axed light
and they detect
voiceovers

telling
how the atolls
glow with pollution
and perfect vaccines.

Qaumaneq

The Inuit have a word for
shaman-light,
but over the tundra
migrating nightingales
fall from the sky

mutations multiply
among snow-lion
and caribou fawn,
white wolf
and lemming

until the shaman,
still stalking local fevers,
lays aside
his radioactive masks,
no longer risks

a dreaming act.

Conjuration

Men conjured Blodeuwedd
from tapers of meadowsweet

Orpheus evoked Eurydice
on the body of the lyre

astronomers, tracking Pluto,
see Persephone

with mourning-jet
at the opiate of her throat

Alcestis wakes – such sugars
work the cist-grave

and Lazarus?
To what voltage

will the five wits lodge
in their living dead?

The nature of the game

It's a long discipline
firing the kiln,
waiting for alchemy
of ash and oxide,
a white glaze
transparent of itself
with no green cast

the fuse and focus
in catching that accidental –
like an intact body
found in a salt-mine –
hermetic, rapt,
the way freshwater
sings in the iceberg.

Momentum

I still remember
the flaxen owl
above the flowing field

the way the wind
took the wheat
between hunter and quarry

the fields around
unmoving,
and mild as paradise.

The impulse

That night in Africa
after the first rains,
we undressed
on the pale-shelving sand,
stood naked and apart.

Suddenly you knelt
beside the phosphorescence
in the rising wave
and laughing
threw lit drops
upon the moonless breasts
you dared not touch.

Looking to Borrowdale

We were snowed up six nights;
each day you composed
an anthem for boys' voices

your expertise
with the virginal
progressions on a naked ground.

So much was bodiless –
the cool half-tones, waking
to snowlight off a sleepless night

that when thaw came
we could no longer pitch
the hot white note

of how our bodies flowed
before the spate.

The blue planet

Monks say
that icons are written
not painted,
the gaze always recycled
between mother and child.

But today
reading their image,
I could see nothing
but the exotic beyond,
blue on blue

the star of the sea
enfolding Buzz Aldrin
as he breaks bread
by earthlight
on the dust of the moon.

Shibui

I keep to the soft greys
of understatement,
for it's not biddable,
the way unrelated things
play havoc,
the contained flame
of a fox on the fire escape.

Its even unsettling
how the dead
hold their own,
and go on reading
under the scratch dial
as if there was no such thing
as innovation.

For this is deep fallow –
a lesser pilgrimage
where snow dumbfounds
and lightweight stars
deploy their solar sails
like blossom
softening a landscape.

After long fallow

(for Belinda King)

It's an orthodox insight –
every seventh year
the land must lie fallow,
even the river
go underground.

Beyond the lilies of the field,
little animals
lean into the wind
as if listening
to its subsong

while we wait
for that rekindling
which conjures
a blue abstract
out of the flax field.

Overspill

(for Sally and Mike)

I sleep in the old granary
under the dovecote
where bats still roost.
I sense their high frequencies
but cannot detect
even a quarter-tone
of any language
to dream in

until at dawn,
when only the light
is irreproachable,
I hear the spilling of grain
and a rising murmur
as the doves
settle once more
into their unsung dust.

The owl window

(for Jennifer and Robert)

The owl's breast
shines in the dark
from roosting in a rotten tree.
Phosphorescence rubs off
on the unglazed circle
under our roof
as it enters
to hunt vermin.

When all but pale roses
go into the night,
I wait for the soft drama
of its heart-valves
over the crooked acres,
until it takes
that luminous O
into the dark.

On opening the north door

(for Elizabeth Temple)

Throw it wide –
the church door above
the grazing marsh
where cattle align themselves
with magnetic north.

Light is the great leveller –
a sweetbread for all souls
against the soft uprising
of things that are not
as though they were.

And silence
is different in sunlight.
The huge hours lean
into that moment
when context is catalyst

Dante drinking
from the water meadows,
exoskeletons
of dragonflies
catching the sun.

Slip between light
and its displacement
like one of those angels
flying below the level
of the crucified

and look north,
where the rainbow
takes its unspilled circle
through poplar and willow
as if treading the light.

The mole-catcher's cottage

(after Ann Arnold)

It was only glimpsed
between a fold of hills,
blue shutters,
hawthorn like hoar-frost poured.

How does it happen
that memory replays
the unseen valley below,
luminous with saplings

one of those landscapes
seething with soft fire
against the principle
of darkness

each puff of pollen
caught through woodsmoke
against the bare hill
of the hawk?

Orkney Epiphany

Read the flow –
sun swinging
between equinoxes

sheep browsing
in salt aureoles
against spelter and gunmetal

rainbows dryfoot
as shoals turn
on a single hinge.

When Magi come,
redden the breast
of the white hare.

The sheep-rustling

No still of the night.
Hot-blooded
clang of metal,
flocks fleeced with steel,
a shower of meteors
grazing the tyre tracks.

Sweat and dew,
vulnerable pigments
of earth-red
and bone-black,
eyes as glass-blanks –
men in balaclavas

or gods
with cloven feet?

In praise of flying squirrels

Understatement is not their thing
as they graze the barbaric blue
like unauthorised gods

theirs is the middle kingdom
below swift and sickle moon,
small drama, with deep focus

their bleached bellies
cross-bandaged
in the diagonal light

until at dusk
the stars let slip
another electric circus.

The elephants of Atlantis

If only I could hear
the elephants of Atlantis
trumpet
through their forests
of liquidambar.

If only I could lift
Shackleton's ship
from its bed of ice,
in full sail
like a bride.

If only I could taste
the vanishing apples;
russets and greenings,
northern spies and seek-no-farthers,
four by fours and hoary mornings.

If only I could watch
the philosopher's stone
condense on the bark of trees,
or the heat shadow of wolves
burn through the juniper.

If only I could free
Merlin from his reliquary
of rippleglass,
and open the eyes of the dead
when their hair is braided.

If only I could catch up
with the rainbow
and those seven herons
dividing the rushes
to the west of nowhere.

If only I could capture
a particle in two places
at once,
or a five-coloured parrot,
or the little dream in red.

If only I could tell
the submariners
that water has a memory
and will call all of them
by their names.

If only, if only
the light would come in
like a different animal,
and the angel serve a small breakfast
in the Electric Palace.

How the snow-leopard became

We can barely detect them –
Rauschenberg's white paintings
where all surface interest
is the shadow of passers-by
falling upon them

or the darker profundity
on Everest, when Mallory
put his snow-goggles in his pocket
as if the light was failing
before he fell

or that moment
when the muzzle of the snow-leopard
comes into mottled focus
and burns
through the blizzard.

Suffolk albatross

It rode the light here once,
in local winds
over coralline crags.

When water rises
in the rainless night,
we still fish the drift

under the exceptional snow
of its wings.

The Queen of Sutton Hoo

They dreamt of her –
the shepherds of Sutton Hoo
as their sheep grazed
the burial mound.

No elbow-room
once shepherd's cress
with its tiny white flowers
took over.

The glitter of beeswax
on her breast
once startled ravens
in the howling blue.

But she has outwitted them all –
the electric queen
wearing gold-foil triangles
in the foxy dark.

The beekeepers

(after Bruegel)

Is it priestcraft they carry
in skeps bound with briar,
robed like divines
with visors of wicker?

And which flightpath
do they follow, hooded
against the secret swarm
no slits for eyes?

The Druids of Primrose Hill

They process
into the autumn equinox,
an archbishop robed,
a brain surgeon
with his wand

past city churches
where the dead
still dispute whether
souls are lightweight
in solid moonlight.

For this is settled land,
with its high-rise
silicon and glass,
the hum of refrigeration,
delicatessens

and when the sun lifts
over bus-lane
and urban foxes,
a kind of giddiness
overcomes me

at the resilience
of this ritual
from the megaliths
while the traffic ticks
as if immortal.

Mountain bikers

How long will it go on –
the lurch of the ski-lift
through mist,
the two of us and a child
suspended under power-lines?

Our bodies lightsome
in this kingdom
of the negligible,
only cow-bells betraying
the invisible beasts.

Then we glimpse them –
eerie bikers, also going up
without horizons,
their machines
slung from the gondola

an oddly muted
travelling circus,
their aerodynamic helmets
heraldic, under the unseen
stations of the sun

stranger than Odin's ravens
flying between past
and future
above the calamitous ground
where we are not saved.

After Ernst

Two children menaced
by a nightingale –
it's partly painting
partly collage.

You cannot predict
the inspiring of terror,
the little wooden gate
moves on real hinges

a masked motor-cyclist
hangs level
with the driving mirror
and will not pass

the boy of the May
crowned between
peeled boughs,
beheaded by Whitsunday.

The lay clerk's song

The angels in the predella
wear slippers
of soft scarlet

Mother of God
let down your
Whitsuntide tresses

I cannot forget
as the boys
ran to the vestry

how light
through the lancet
knelt

at their nakedness.

Sea-otter and child

St Cuthbert is sitting
out of the wind,
on ancient waves of shingle,
reading the discipline
of the Rule.

Looking up, he sees
the foil of creatures
over sand,
jouissance
of otters at play

and for a moment
in supple light
against an ebb-tide,
the sun
suspends its cymbal.

Our Lady of the dry tree

(after Petrus Christus)

Fifteenth century –
mother and child
embraced by thorns
on a tiny oak panel.

No electric diadems –
but they burn
in the difficult light
as if their barren tree
were still vivid
with sap.

Krishna and the milkmaids

They wear silk
sheer as woven wind,
while the bells sewn
into their hems
sound like colours
in rippled water.

Between the Indian yellows
and jungle fowl
with feathered feet,
he can see cows
fed only on mangoes
cross the bridge
and its outbreath

but not until dusk –
that kneeling donor
in a blue cowl –
do the nightingales
in the tamarisk
break cover
and female moths
secrete light.

Outsleeping the monsoon

In the purple foothills,
the little hours
run on light feet
like spotted deer
in the fallow dark

leopard geckos
and sugar-gliders
doze in underwater light
to the sound
of the rain ceasing

mustard fields
become lakes of sulphur,
the mango orchards
smoke, like a magical
apparatus

until unbidden,
a yellow blind
is released at the back
of a sequence of rooms
and the lovers emerge

unfazed as swifts
sleeping in flight.

The dislocation

We neither come nor depart
but float,
like those live fish
in the carafe
on the dining-table

the hotel corridors deserted,
the lotus lifting
from its stem
as dancing girls
plead paradise.

We make our own rituals;
walking meditation,
beer in frosted glasses,
a three-coloured cat
bringing happiness

take forays
to the scissor-shop,
the purple forbidden city,
a Vietnamese wedding
where dry ice rises

and glimmering petals
fall into a pool
of heart-shaped balloons
as the bride changes
into a scarlet dress.

On the Red river
dragon prows
have coals in their jaws,
cranes glide past,
the containers hesitate.

Have we made
a miscalculation
while lying
in limbo beside
the blue salamander?

For a glass shutter
has come down,
parakeets shriek
in the strangler fig,
the air-conditioning roars

and we neither come nor depart.

Insight

After the ammonia attack,
my left eye
was burned shut.
But I saw with the other
that even the heart is off-centre.

Once, the cherubim were all eyes.
Under carved angels
the priest brought animal membranes
for rebels dying
from their wounds.

Now my stem-cells are grown
on a tissue of amniotic sac,
transplanted
like gold-beater's skin
to my cornea.

I wait for two months
and think of this gift
from a Caesarean,
how we are both smitten
and hallowed.

As the cells multiply,
I see the flicker-shadow
of beech leaves
shaking out
their green samite

and the insight
of the swallow
passing one of his long tail feathers
under the Virgin's eyelid
to remove grit.

George Herbert plays the lute

It's a Japanese way of looking –
notes catching like fireflies,
the singing men of Sarum
seeing the silence between sounds
shake its magical apparel,
intimate, intemperate,
like snow along the vein.

The sounding

It was dumbshow,
a bird's wing protruding
from the organ-pipe
between stiff sheaves
of lilies

but the stopped note –
that moment
when memory
takes a slip of time
and strikes it

was its far cry
a god's mouth
rinsed out
with sulphur,
tamarisk

or simply
how death
the nightingale
once wintered
in your throat?

Overwintering

Light and its loss.
Each day
a guessing game,
the snow which fell
several centuries ago
everything and nothing.

Thaw
almost within earshot,
sigh of an axe
in its antler-sleeve,
passwords pronounced
by the dead

a girl buried
with flowering yarrow
and three crab-apples,
as if her breasts
were still giddy
with milk

the vanishing point
a wave of cherry blossom
moving through memory
until we are dazed
by the slow pollen
the gradual dazzle.

Onsen

A tub of cedar-wood,
Japanese girls
dense as flowers,
the easy mystery of
their thighs glimpsed
through resinous steam.

Above painted finches
on the bamboo screen,
sky, ribboned
with vapour-trails,
a huge wind-turbine,
the hum of elsewhere.

I lean back
in the commingled
light and water
and wonder which
the more mysterious –
soft-focus between horizons

or that act of metaphor,
the going-under.

The wedding at Valletta

We look down
from the balcony
on the Barrakka gardens
where women wear
fascinators
that quiver like humming-birds
in the hot wind off the sea.

Tankers ghost the horizon,
dredgers glide by,
derricks of gamboge-yellow
straddle the dry dock
as children untether
white balloons
on the forbidden grass.

Three soldiers
in light khaki and white helmets
trot out, like little goats
with ignition strips and lantern
at the preposterous
priming of canons
for the bridal couple.

Beyond, little pavilions
of ribbon and organza
glimmer against
the isolation hospital,
where knights of St John
once walked the steps
in heavy armour.

It's dizzying –
the sun's ecliptic
through resounding blue,
the crackle of matter,
static of the bride's
cream silk, that treachery
of perception

which once turned
water into wine.

Rimbaud in Zanzibar

It was intravenous
as opium –
the scent of cloves
over the sea,
humming-birds
migrating thousands
of miles,
the scarlet
from distant atrocities.

And when he saw
drowned slaves
still wearing their manacles,
did it ever return,
that remorseless moment
when he relinquished
all blazing metaphors
and looking up, saw
the sun lightheaded
in its crucible?

Apothecary's song

Quaking-grass
for the heart's tremor

saffron-crocus
for the skin scarified

blue-trembled flax
for scourging

moth-mullein
to staunch haemorrhage

hyssop
at the wound's lip

and scattered like dice,
fritillary

snakeshead
under the Judas tree.

A Kind of Quickening

Put your ear to the quoins.
You might think
a redundant church
would be loud
with the sound of silence,
but sacred cantatas
rise to the spandrels.

Look through the squint.
St Mary-at-the-Quay
in her field of windscreens,
where crane-drivers
glide over the hammerbeams
as if sighting eternity
seawards.

Smell the mown grass
in the roofless nave,
when children circle-dance
like Wisdom before the Lord
until the sea-fret rolls in
and they pull up
their pearled hoods.

And the weepers on the tomb –
do they look up
in sunlight
as we repair the fabric,
salt-laden limestone,
an altar frontal
transfigured by the silkworm?

We still celebrate
the energy of otherness.
That shadow on
the lime-washed chancel
not simply Christ
as makeweight
on the flowering tree

but a jazz-singer,
dress blue as hyssop
against the downbeat dusk,
while on the sky line
wind-turbines turn
to the preaching
of the swallow.

Long Friday

1

Small sun through mist,
five turbines in silverpoint
blades turning, turning,
a swish as of walking
through long grass.

Then the eerie shift
of something unfinished,
flicker-shadow,
the uncoordinated wounds
of Christ.

2

Crucifixion,
a centurion
gazing up at the body
with its crown
of razor-wire

transfixed by
that shimmer
in zero sunlight –
incarnation,
the dove

in the double helix.

The key and the crystal

Snowflakes
fernlike, stellar

falling so slowly
they seem stationary

I watch them
come into focus

each a latchkey
to language

its bright anxiety
never repeated.